A Child's Book of Psalms

STAMPLEY

PRODUCED BY C4CI, BELGIUM
PUBLISHED EXCLUSIVELY IN ENGLISH AND SPANISH BY:
C.D. Stampley Enterprises, Inc., Charlotte NC, USA Email: info@stampley.com
ISBN 978-1-58087-124-2 • Code 0379
Printed in China – 2007.

www.stampley.com

*T*ABLE OF CONTENTS

INTRODUCTION 7

PSALMS OF PRAISE
Psalms 8, 19, 98, 100, 104, 113, 148, 150

God honors man **11**

Heaven reveals God **12**

Sing praise to God **14**

God, worthy of all praise **17**

God sustains and cares for us **19**

God exalts the faithful **21**

All praise God **22**

Let us happily praise God **25**

PSALMS OF THANKSGIVING
Psalms 30, 103, 107, 118, 138

God frees us from danger **34**

Thanksgiving for God's goodness **37**

God frees those who seek Him **38**

Blessings in trusting God **40**

God heeds and saves the humble **43**

PSALMS OF PETITION
Psalms 22, 51

Prayer in time of need **44**

Prayer for God's mercy **47**

PSALMS OF TRUST
Psalms 18, 23, 27, 67

Hymn of gratitude and victory **26**

The Lord, the good shepherd **29**

The Lord is our light **30**

God shall bless us **33**

PSALMS OF WISDOM
Psalm 1, 37, 119

Happiness of the just **48**

The just are blessed by God **51**

Blessing for following the Law of God **52**

THE STORY OF DAVID 54

GOD'S COVENANT WITH HIS PEOPLE 58

MAP AND TIMELINE 60

Sing unto the LORD with the harp;
with the harp, and the voice of a psalm.

Psalm 98:5

PSALMS: INTRODUCTION

By Amy Welborn

People have lots of different ways of praying to God, don't they? Sometimes we pray alone, and a lot of times we pray with other people. Sometimes we pray aloud and sometimes we just sit quietly and listen to God. Sometimes we talk to God in our own words, and sometimes we use prayers that other people have written. They can help us, too.

There's one collection of prayers that people around the world have been praying for a very long time – thousands of years! These prayers are called the Psalms.

What are the Psalms?

The Psalms are prayers about the people of Israel's relationship with God. There are 150 of them in all. They are divided into five different sections. The Psalms were originally written in Hebrew, the language the Jewish people used when they worshipped God.

The 150 Psalms we have today were written over hundreds of years. The oldest Psalms were written by King David over three thousand years ago, in the 10th century BC.

The word "psalm" had more than one meaning in ancient times. It could refer to the strumming of a musical instrument of some kind, or it could mean just "song." This gives us a hint about what kind of prayers the Psalms were: they were songs!

You don't have to sing the Psalms when you pray them, of course, and ancient people didn't sing or chant them all the time either. But singing them in the Temple and then in the synagogues was the most important way the Jewish people prayed the Psalms. You can tell that the Psalms were meant for singing because several of them have notes about what musical instruments or types of voices should be used when praying them.

What are the Psalms about?

The people of Israel loved God very much. He was the center of their lives, every day. They knew that God had created each one of them and loved them. They also knew that God had adopted them as His special, Chosen People. God had made a covenant with them and promised to protect them. They promised to obey God's Law and be a light to the nations.

The Psalms are prayers that tell the whole story of Israel and God. In these prayers, the people of Israel tell God how much they love Him and how thankful they are. They are happy and full of joy.

But like everyone else, the people of Israel went through hard times. They lost the land God had given them. They turned away from God. They wondered if God would help them, and they were sad and confused, even angry. The Psalms tell that part of the story, too.

This book divides the Psalms into five different kinds:

Psalms of Praise: When we pray these Psalms, we praise God for Creation (Ps. 8), the Law He gives us to live by (Ps. 19), and the best reason of all: being God (Ps. 104).

The Psalms of Praise are joyful, with everyone invited to join in the praise – every kind of person, using every kind of musical instrument. It's a joyful celebration!

Psalms of Trust: The people of Israel trusted that God would help through hard times. These Psalms helped them to be strong, to remember God's promise to give them strength, and to not be afraid of evil (Ps. 18), the shadow of death (Ps. 23) or any kind of enemy at all (Ps. 27).

Psalms of Thanksgiving: Every day gives us new reasons to thank God. The Psalms are full of thanksgiving! The people of Israel thanked God for making them happy (Ps. 30), for freeing them from slavery (Ps. 107) and forgiving their sins (Ps. 107).

Psalms of Petition: God loves us and wants to help us – we just have to ask Him! Through the Psalms, we can pray to God, asking Him to help us when we're having a hard time (Ps. 22) and to forgive us when we've done something wrong (Ps. 51).

Psalms of Wisdom: God made us and knows what will make us happy. There are Psalms thanking God for the wisdom to know His plan for us. They are reminders that it's God that makes us happy, not anything else (Ps. 1), and prayers asking Him to help us stay on that path and live in His light (Ps. 119).

How Do I Pray the Psalms?

The Psalms are amazing because people have been praying them non-stop, around the world, for thousands of years. They're the oldest prayers that Christians and Jews can pray.

You can pray the Psalms by reading them quietly or aloud. Sometimes people like to read them together, each person taking their turn to read two lines at a time, back and forth. You could even make up your own tune for your favorite Psalm!

When we pray, we talk and listen to God. Sometimes we use our own words, and that's great. But sometimes it helps us to use prayers that other people have written, too. They put into words feelings and thoughts that we can't. The Psalms are good for that because no matter how you feel, you can find a Psalm to match it!

When you pray the Psalms, you're joining a big group: millions of boys and girls, men and women, who over thousands of years have prayed and sung these words because, just like you, they love God.

PSALM 8

God honors man

When I consider thy heavens, the work of thy fingers,
    the moon and the stars, which thou hast ordained;

What is man, that thou art mindful of him?
    and the son of man, that thou visitest him?

For thou hast made him a little lower than the angels,
    and hast crowned him with glory and honour.

Thou madest him to have dominion over the works of
    thy hands; thou hast put all things under his feet:

All sheep and oxen, yea, and the beasts of the field;

The fowl of the air, and the fish of the sea, and
    whatsoever passeth through the paths of the seas.

O Lord our Lord, how excellent is thy name in all
    the earth!

(Verses 3–9)

PSALM 19
Heaven reveals God

The heavens declare the glory of God; and the firmament sheweth his handywork.

Day unto day uttereth speech, and night unto night sheweth knowledge.

There is no speech nor language, where their voice is not heard.

Their line is gone out through all the earth, and their words to the end of the world.

The law of the LORD is perfect, converting the soul: the testimony of the LORD is sure, making wise the simple.

More to be desired are they than gold, yea, than much fine gold: sweeter also than honey and the honeycomb.

Moreover by them is thy servant warned: and in keeping of them there is great reward.

(Verses 1–3, 4a, 7, 10, 11)

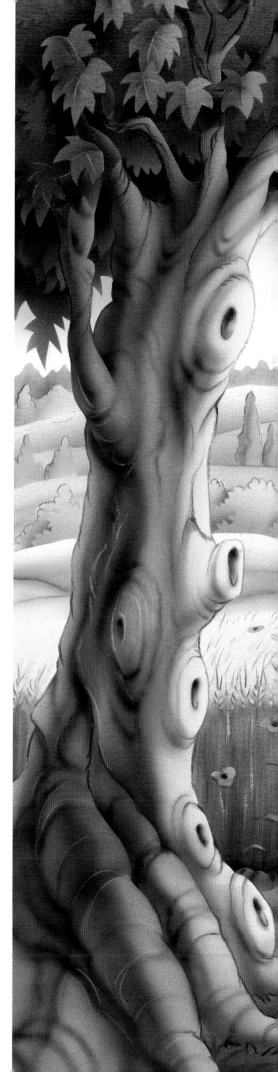

PSALM 98

Sing praise to God

O sing unto the LORD a new song; for he hath done marvellous things: his right hand, and his holy arm, hath gotten him the victory.

The LORD hath made known his salvation: his righteousness hath he openly shewed in the sight of the heathen.

He hath remembered his mercy and his truth toward the house of Israel: all the ends of the earth have seen the salvation of our God.

Make a joyful noise unto the LORD, all the earth: make a loud noise, and rejoice, and sing praise.

Sing unto the LORD with the harp; with the harp, and the voice of a psalm.

With trumpets and sound of cornet make a joyful noise before the LORD, the king.

(Verses 1–6)

PSALM 100

God, worthy of all praise

Make a joyful noise unto the LORD, all ye lands.

Serve the LORD with gladness: come before his presence with singing.

Know ye that the LORD he is God: it is he that hath made us, and not we ourselves; we are his people, and the sheep of his pasture.

Enter into his gates with thanksgiving, and into his courts with praise: be thankful unto him, and bless his name.

For the LORD is good; his mercy is everlasting; and his truth endureth to all generations.

PSALM 104
God sustains and cares for us

Bless the LORD, O my soul. O LORD my God,
   thou art very great; thou art clothed with honour
   and majesty.

He sendeth the springs into the valleys, which run
   among the hills.

They give drink to every beast of the field: the wild
   asses quench their thirst.

By them shall the fowls of the heaven have their
   habitation, which sing among the branches.

He watereth the hills from his chambers: the earth is
   satisfied with the fruit of thy works.

He causeth the grass to grow for the cattle, and herb for
   the service of man: that he may bring forth food out
   of the earth;

O LORD, how manifold are thy works! in wisdom hast
   thou made them all: the earth is full of thy riches.

(Verses 1, 10–14, 24)

19

PSALM 113
God exalts the faithful

Praise ye the LORD. Praise, O ye servants of the LORD, praise the name of the LORD.

Blessed be the name of the LORD from this time forth and for evermore.

Who is like unto the LORD our God, who dwelleth on high,

Who humbleth himself to behold the things that are in heaven, and in the earth!

He raiseth up the poor out of the dust, and lifteth the needy out of the dunghill;

That he may set him with princes, even with the princes of his people.

He maketh the barren woman to keep house, and to be a joyful mother of children. Praise ye the LORD.

(Verses 1–2, 5–9)

$\mathscr{P}$SALM 148
All praise God

Praise the LORD from the earth, ye dragons,
and all deeps:

Fire, and hail; snow, and vapours; stormy wind fulfilling
his word:

Mountains, and all hills; fruitful trees, and all cedars:

Beasts, and all cattle; creeping things, and flying fowl:

Kings of the earth, and all people; princes, and all
judges of the earth:

Both young men, and maidens; old men, and children:

Let them praise the name of the LORD: for his name
alone is excellent; his glory is above the earth
and heaven.

(Verses 7–13)

22

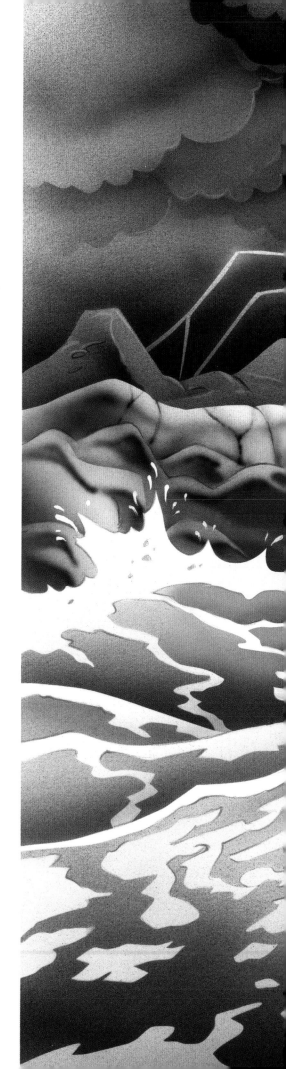

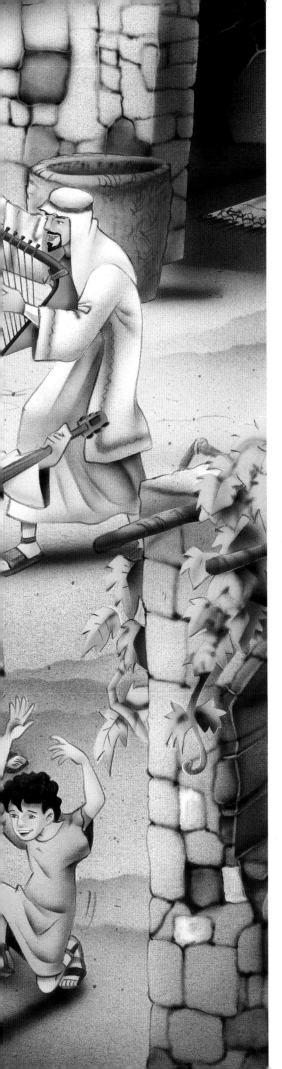

PSALM 150
Let us happily praise God

Praise ye the LORD. Praise God in his sanctuary: praise him in the firmament of his power.

Praise him for his mighty acts: praise him according to his excellent greatness.

Praise him with the sound of the trumpet: praise him with the psaltery and harp.

Praise him with the timbrel and dance: praise him with stringed instruments and organs.

Praise him upon the loud cymbals: praise him upon the high sounding cymbals.

Let every thing that hath breath praise the LORD. Praise ye the LORD.

PSALM 18
Hymn of gratitude and victory

I will love thee, O LORD, my strength.

The LORD is my rock, and my fortress, and my deliverer; my God, my strength, in whom I will trust; my buckler, and the horn of my salvation, and my high tower.

As for God, his way is perfect: the word of the LORD is tried: he is a buckler to all those that trust in him.

For who is God save the LORD? or who is a rock save our God?

It is God that girdeth me with strength, and maketh my way perfect.

He maketh my feet like hind's feet, and setteth me upon my high places.

Thou hast also given me the shield of thy salvation: and thy right hand hath holden me up, and thy gentleness hath made me great.

(Verses 1, 2, 30–33, 35)

PSALM 23
The LORD, the good shepherd

The LORD is my sheperd; I shall not want.

He maketh me to lie down in green pastures: he leadeth me beside the still waters.

He restoreth my soul: he leadeth me in the paths of righteousness for his name's sake.

Yea, though I walk through the valley of the shadow of death, I will fear no evil: for thou art with me; thy rod and thy staff they comfort me.

Thou preparest a table before me in the presence of mine enemies: thou anointest my head with oil; my cup runneth over.

Surely goodness and mercy shall follow me all the days of my life: and I will dwell in the house of the LORD for ever.

PSALM 27

The LORD is our light

The LORD is my light and my salvation; whom shall I fear? the LORD is the strength of my life; of whom shall I be afraid?

Though an host should encamp against me, my heart shall not fear: though war should rise against me, in this will I be confident.

One thing have I desired of the LORD, that will I seek after; that I may dwell in the house of the LORD all the days of my life, to behold the beauty of the LORD, and to enquire in his temple.

For in the time of trouble he shall hide me in his pavilion: in the secret of his tabernacle shall he hide me; he shall set me up upon a rock.

And now shall mine head be lifted up above mine enemies round about me: therefore will I offer in his tabernacle sacrifices of joy; I will sing, yea, I will sing praises unto the LORD.

(Verses 1, 3–6)

PSALM 67

God shall bless us

God be merciful unto us, and bless us; and cause his face to shine upon us; Selah.

That thy way may be known upon earth, thy saving health among all nations.

Let the people praise thee, O God; let all the people praise thee.

O let the nations be glad and sing for joy: for thou shalt judge the people righteously, and govern the nations upon earth. Selah.

Let the people praise thee, O God; let all the people praise thee.

Then shall the earth yield her increase; and God, even our own God, shall bless us.

God shall bless us, and all the ends of the earth shall fear him.

𝒫SALM 30

God frees us from danger

I will extol thee, O Lord; for thou hast lifted me up,
 and hast not made my foes to rejoice over me.

O Lord my God, I cried unto thee, and thou hast
 healed me.

Oh Lord, thou hast brought up my soul from the grave:
 thou hast kept me alive, that I should not go down to
 the pit.

Sing unto the Lord, O ye saints of his, and give thanks
 at the remembrance of his holiness.

For his anger endureth but a moment; in his favour is
 life: weeping may endure for a night, but joy cometh
 in the morning.

Thou hast turned for me my mourning into dancing:
 thou hast put off my sackcloth, and girded me
 with gladness;

To the end that my glory may sing praise to thee, and
 not be silent. O Lord my God, I will give thanks
 unto thee for ever.

(Verses 1–5, 11, 12)

PSALM 103
Thanksgiving for God's goodness

Bless the LORD, O my soul: and all that is within me,
   bless his holy name.

Bless the LORD, O my soul, and forget not all his benefits:

Who forgiveth all thine iniquities; who healeth
   all thy diseases;

Who redeemeth thy life from destruction; who crowneth

   thee with lovingkindness and tender mercies;

Who satisfieth thy mouth with good things; so that thy
   youth is renewed like the eagle's.

The LORD executeth righteousness and judgement for
   all that are oppressed.

He made known his ways unto Moses,
   his acts unto the children of Israel.

The LORD is merciful and gracious, slow to anger, and
   plenteous in mercy.

(Verses 1–8)

37

PSALM 107

God frees those who seek Him

O give thanks unto the Lord, for he is good: for his mercy endureth for ever.

Let the redeemed of the Lord say so, whom he hath redeemed from the hand of the enemy;

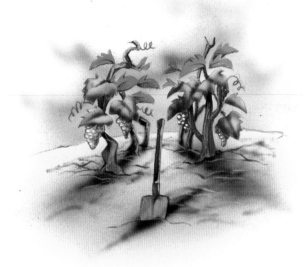

And gathered them out of the lands, from the east, and from the west, from the north, and from the south.

They wandered in the wilderness in a solitary way; they found no city to dwell in.

Hungry and thirsty, their soul fainted in them.

Then they cried unto the Lord in their trouble, and he delivered them out of their distresses.

And he led them forth by the right way, that they might go to a city of habitation.

Oh that men would praise the Lord for his goodness, and for his wonderful works to the children of men!

For he satisfieth the longing soul, and filleth the hungry soul with goodness.

(Verses 1–9)

PSALM 118

Blessings in trusting God

I called upon the LORD in distress: the LORD answered me, and set me in a large place.

The LORD is on my side; I will not fear: what can man do unto me?

The LORD taketh my part with them that help me: therefore shall I see my desire upon them that hate me.

It is better to trust in the LORD than to put confidence in man.

It is better to trust in the LORD than to put confidence in princes.

Open to me the gates of righteousness: I will go into them, and I will praise the LORD:

I will praise thee: for thou hast heard me, and art become my salvation.

(Verses 5–9, 19, 21)

PSALM 138
God heeds and saves the humble

All the kings of the earth shall praise thee, O LORD, when they hear the words of thy mouth.

Yea, they shall sing in the ways of the LORD: for great is the glory of the LORD.

Though the LORD be high, yet hath he respect unto the lowly: but the proud he knoweth afar off.

Though I walk in the midst of trouble, thou wilt revive me: thou shalt stretch forth thine hand against the wrath of mine enemies, and thy right hand shall save me.

The LORD will perfect that which concerneth me: thy mercy, O LORD, endureth for ever: forsake not the works of thine own hands.

(Verses 4–8)

PSALM 22

Prayer in time of need

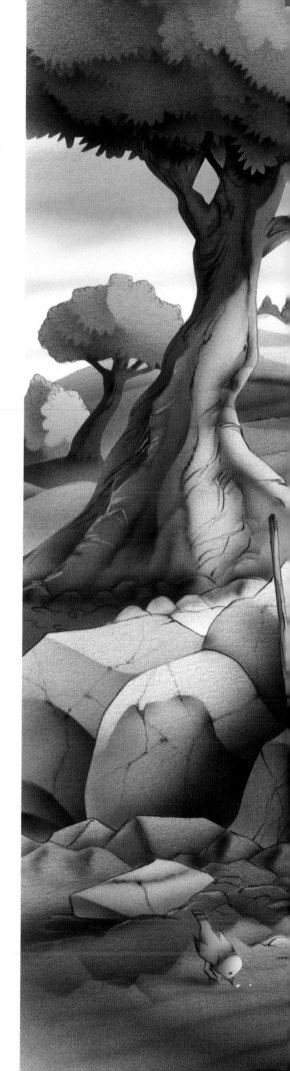

My God, my God, why hast thou forsaken me? why art thou so far from helping me, and from the words of my roaring?

O my God, I cry in the daytime, but thou hearest not; and in the night season, and am not silent.

But thou art holy, O thou that inhabitest the praises of Israel.

Our fathers trusted in thee: they trusted, and thou didst deliver them.

I was cast upon thee from the womb: thou art my God from my mother's belly.

Be not far from me; for trouble is near; for there is none to help.

But be not thou far from me, O LORD: O my strength, haste thee to help me.

(Verses 1–4, 10, 11, 19)

PSALM 51
Prayer for God's mercy

Have mercy upon me, O God, according to thy lovingkindness: according unto the multitude of thy tender mercies blot out my transgressions.

Wash me thoroughly from mine iniquity, and cleanse me from my sin.

For I acknowledge my transgressions: and my sin is ever before me.

Purge me with hyssop, and I shall be clean: wash me, and I shall be whiter than snow.

Hide thy face from my sins, and blot out all mine iniquities.

Create in me a clean heart, O God; and renew a right spirit within me.

(Verses 1–3, 7, 9, 10)

SALM 1

Happiness of the just

Blessed is the man that walketh not in the counsel of the ungodly, nor standeth in the way of sinners, nor sitteth in the seat of the scornful.

But his delight is in the law of the LORD; and in his law doth he meditate day and night.

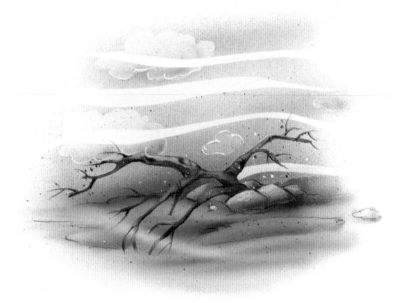

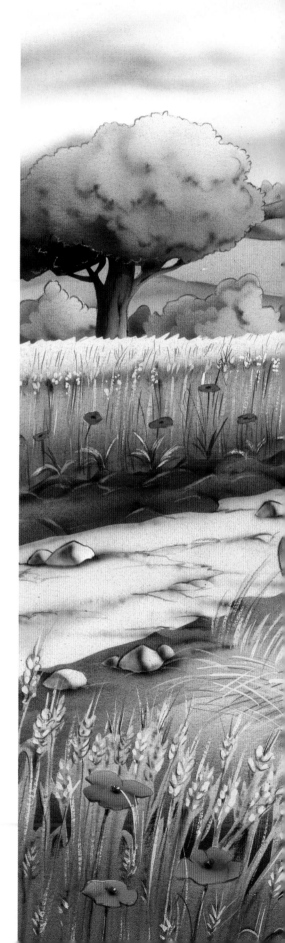

And he shall be like a tree planted by the rivers of water, that bringeth forth his fruit in his season; his leaf also shall not wither; and whatsoever he doeth shall prosper.

The ungodly are not so: but are like the chaff which the wind driveth away.

Therefore the ungodly shall not stand in the judgment, nor sinners in the congregation of the righteous.

For the LORD knoweth the way of the righteous: but the way of the ungodly shall perish.

PSALM 37

The just are blessed by God

Trust in the LORD, and do good; so shalt thou dwell in the land, and verily thou shalt be fed.

Delight thyself also in the LORD; and he shall give thee the desires of thine heart.

Commit thy way unto the LORD; trust also in him; and he shall bring it to pass.

And he shall bring forth thy righteousness as the light, and thy judgment as the noonday.

Rest in the LORD, and wait patiently for him: fret not thyself because of him who prospereth in his way, because of the man who bringeth wicked devices to pass.

Cease from anger, and forsake wrath: fret not thyself in any wise to do evil.

For evildoers shall be cut off: but those that wait upon the LORD, they shall inherit the earth.

For yet a little while, and the wicked shall not be: yea, thou shalt diligently consider his place, and it shall not be.

But the meek shall inherit the earth; and shall delight themselves in the abundance of peace.

(Verses 3–11)

51

𝒫SALM 119

Blessing for following the Law of God

Blessed art thou, O LORD: teach me thy statues.

With my lips have I declared all the judgments
of thy mouth.

I have rejoiced in the way of thy testimonies, as much as
in all riches.

I will meditate in thy precepts, and have respect unto
thy ways.

Teach me, O LORD, the way of thy statutes; and I shall
keep it unto the end.

Give me understanding, and I shall keep thy law;
yea, I shall observe it with my whole heart.

Make me to go in the path of thy commandments; for
therein do I delight.

Incline my heart unto thy testimonies,
and not to covetousness.

O how I love thy law! it is my meditation all the day.

Thy word is a lamp unto my feet, and a light unto
my path.

(Verses 12–15, 33–36, 97, 105)

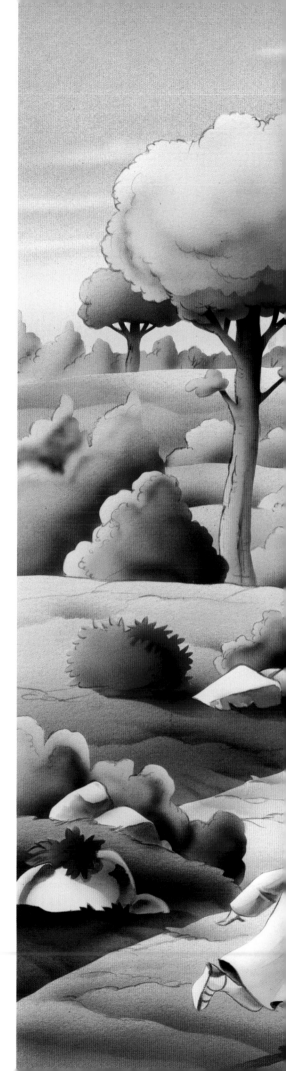

THE STORY OF DAVID

By Amy Welborn

Before he was a great king, David was just a shepherd boy.

One day a prophet named Samuel came to Jesse, David's father. God had told Samuel that he would find a new king for Israel among Jesse's sons. So Samuel went to see Jesse, and Jesse called each of his sons to meet him. But God told Samuel that none of these big, strong men was the one.

Finally, David, the youngest, came in from the fields. God told Samuel that here, finally, was the one He was choosing to be king.

Everyone was surprised because David was so young. But that's the way God is: He never does what we expect!

Now at this time Israel already had a king named Saul. But Saul was troubled and sometimes disobeyed God. King Saul heard that the boy David was a good musician who played the harp and sang beautifully. He asked David to come play for him, and that helped Saul feel better when he was sad and upset.

One day, when David was still young, some enemies called the Philistines challenged the army of Israel. They said that their fight would be settled by one of their soldiers, a giant named Goliath. They were sure the mighty Goliath would defeat any soldier Israel would send.

David volunteered. David surprised everyone because he wouldn't even wear armor. But he took Goliath down with a single stone flung from his slingshot. David knew that God was with him, and he trusted God to give him strength.

As David grew up, he became such a good soldier that King Saul grew very jealous of David, and started trying to kill him.

One night, David saw that Saul and his men were sleeping in a cave. David was able to sneak in, right next to Saul. He could have killed Saul right then, but he didn't. Instead he cut off part of Saul's cape and then from a distance, told him

what he had done. He asked Saul to please stop chasing him and to let God be the judge between them.

For a while, Saul agreed, but later he grew more and more angry and confused. He eventually died in battle, asking one of his own men to kill him, a very sad end.

Now David was king. He brought all of God's tribes together, made Jerusalem the capital of Israel and brought the special chest that held the Ten Commandments, the Ark of the Covenant, there.

It was a great celebration when David brought the Ark to Jerusalem. He danced and sang in front of it and led all the people in praise to God. Some people – including his wife – didn't like to see David dancing and singing like that, but David didn't care. He wanted to praise God.

David did many good things for Israel, but he also did one very bad thing. He fell in love with a woman named Bathsheba, who was married to a man named Uriah. David had Uriah sent to the frontlines of a battle so he would be killed and

David could have Bathsheba all to himself.

The prophet of God named Nathan came to David and told him what a terrible sin he had committed. David was very sorry and humbled himself to show God how sorry he was.

We remember David as a great king who listened to God and wanted to follow God, even though sometimes he failed badly.

We believe that David wrote seventy-three of the Psalms, and you can meet him there. There are Psalms where we read of a king especially chosen by God to help lead His people on earth. David fought many battles, and some of the Psalms are prayers for strength in battle. Once he realized his great sin, David didn't wait to tell God he was sorry. There are Psalms that help us tell God we're sorry, too.

Most of all, when we pray the Psalms, we're doing something very special: We're joining with David, who danced with joy in front of God's Ark, and who sat in the fields as a boy, playing his harp. We're raising our voices with his, singing praise to God!

GOD'S COVENANT WITH HIS PEOPLE

By Amy Welborn

Many years ago, a man named Abram lived in the Middle East. He was a good man with a family and a full life. God called Abram, and told him he was being chosen. Why?

God was choosing Abram to be the father of a special people – God's own Chosen People. God made a covenant, or agreement, with Abram. God would protect Abram and give him a homeland and a great family as numerous as the stars in the sky. Abram agreed that he and his family would always be faithful to God. God then changed Abram's name to "Abraham" as a sign of his new life.

That's how the story of God's people, called Israel or the Jewish people, began. They were chosen by God to show the world how much God loves us and how loving God and living according to His Law brings happiness.

Abraham led his family to the Promised Land, now called Israel. Many years later, though, the people of Israel became slaves in Egypt. God called another leader, Moses, to lead them out of slavery back to the Promised Land.

God gave His people the Law – the Ten Commandments and many other laws – that taught them how to live in peace and happiness. The people of Israel treasured the Ten Commandments, and placed them in a beautifully decorated chest called the Ark of the Covenant. When David's son Solomon finally built a Temple in Jerusalem, the Ark of the Covenant was placed there, and the people honored it as a special way that God was present among them.

This is the world of the Psalms. The Psalms are the prayers of God's people who know how much God has done for them. They knew that it was God who called Abraham and made him their father in faith. It was God who rescued them from slavery, and gave them the wisdom of the Law. It was God who protected them from their enemies. It was God who gave them a king to lead them. And it was God who promised that some day, goodness and peace would last forever.

The Psalms are filled with joy and hope. The people who prayed them centuries ago were happy at being in God's presence in His Temple in Jerusalem. When they prayed about being happy forever, they thought about it as if they would be in the Temple always.

God's people were afraid of real enemies who tried to take the land He had promised them. When they prayed the Psalms they asked God to protect them. They knew that God had given them the Law for their own happiness, and they were sorry when they disobeyed. By praying the Psalms, they recalled how God had rescued them from slavery and said how sorry they were for the times they forgot God's kindness.

Most of all, they knew how wonderful God was – that He had rescued them, again and again, from sadness and pain. They had much to be thankful for – and in the Psalms, they sang those thanks to God!

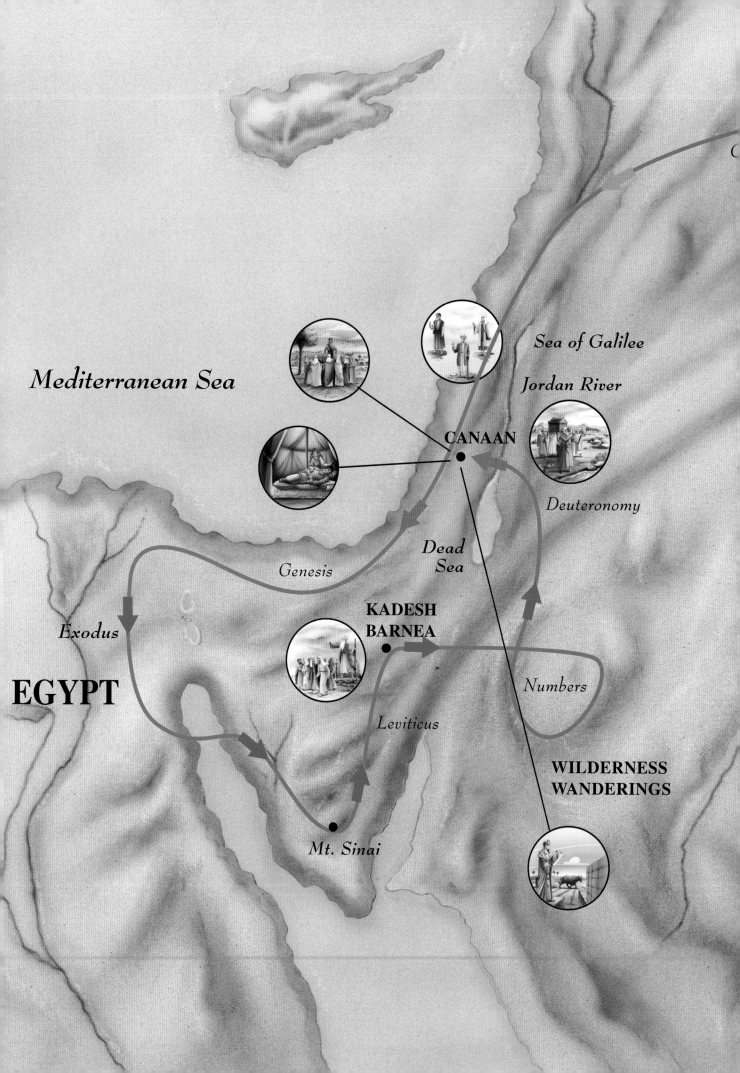

Mediterranean Sea

Sea of Galilee

Jordan River

CANAAN

Deuteronomy

Genesis

Dead
Sea

Exodus

KADESH
BARNEA

EGYPT

Numbers

Leviticus

WILDERNESS
WANDERINGS

Mt. Sinai

MAP AND TIMELINE

Euphrates River

ABRAHAM LEAVES UR
God tells Abram to leave Ur for Canaan (Israel). God changes Abram's name to Abraham, and promises him many descendants.
c. 2200 BC

ISAAC, JACOB, JOSEPH
God's promise to Abraham is fulfilled with the birth of his son, Isaac. Issac fathers Jacob and Jacob's sons give rise to the twelve Tribes of Israel.
c. 2176 – 1876 BC

MOSES AND THE EXODUS
The People of Israel migrate to Egypt and are later enslaved. Moses leads them out of Egypt and into the desert for 40 years.
c. 1501 – 1405 BC

JOSHUA AND THE RETURN TO CANAAN
After Moses dies Joshua leads the Israelites. God, present in the Ark of the Covenant, parts the Jordan River so His people can return home.
c. 1405 BC

THE TIME OF THE JUDGES
For a time the Israelites have no king and are ruled instead by Judges. Samson is a famous Judge of Israel.
c. 1350 – 1042 BC

DAVID BECOMES KING
Saul is the first king of Israel. But Saul displeases God, who then choses David as Israel's new king.
c. 1010 BC

SOLOMON BUILDS THE TEMPLE
David's son Solomon becomes king. He builds a great Temple to honor God and to house the Ark of the Covenant.
c. 959 BC